SCHIRMER'S LIBRARY
OF MUSICAL CLASSICS

Vol. 2072

FRÉDÉRIC CHOPIN

Favorite Piano Works

12 Nocturnes, 8 Etudes, 10 Preludes, 12 Waltzes

16 Mazurkas, 3 Polonaises, 4 Other Pieces

ISBN 978-1-4234-3135-0

G. SCHIRMER, Inc.

DISTRIBUTED BY

HAL•LEONARD®
CORPORATION

7777 W. BLUEMOUND RD. P.O. BOX 13819 MILWAUKEE, WI 53213

www.schirmer.com
www.halleonard.com

Contents

Nocturnes

Etudes

Preludes

WALTZES

MAZURKAS

POLONAISES

à Madame Camilla Pleyel

NOCTURNE
in E-flat Major

Frédéric Chopin
Op. 9, No. 2

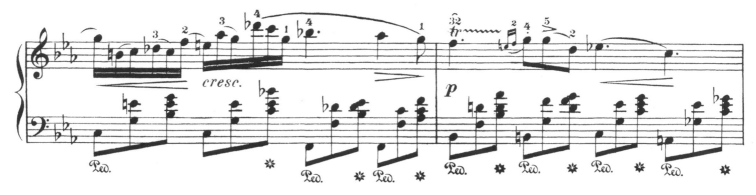

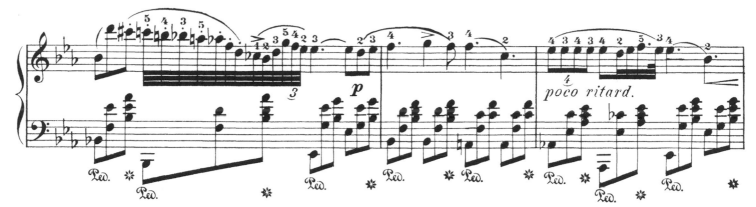

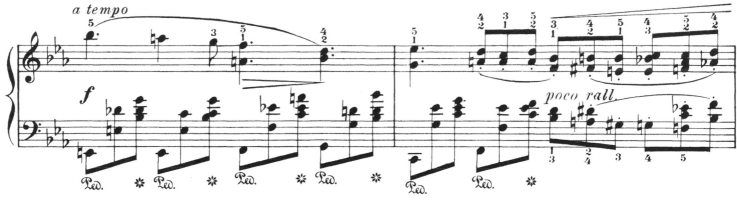

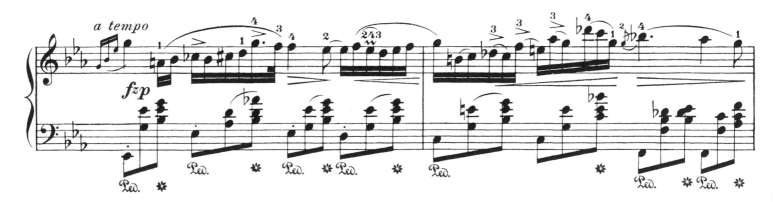

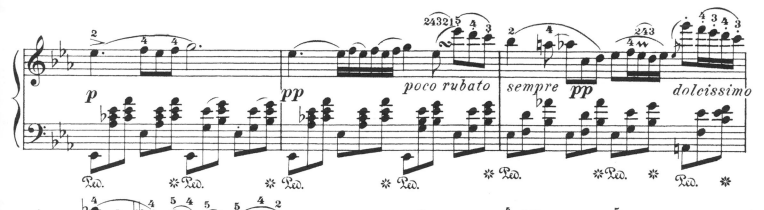

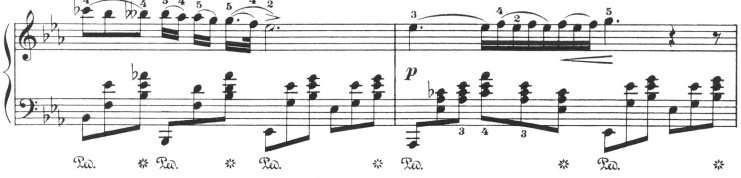

à Monsieur Ferdinand Hiller

NOCTURNE
in F-sharp Major

Frédéric Chopin
Op. 15, No. 2

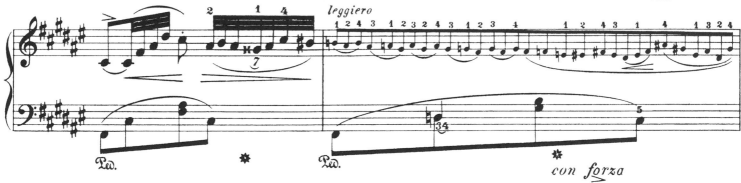

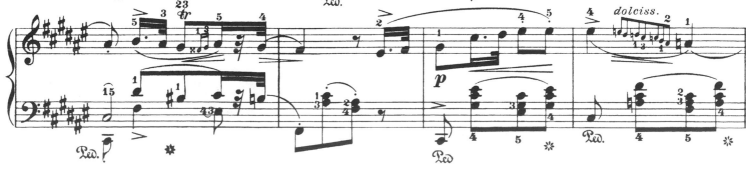

Doppio movimento

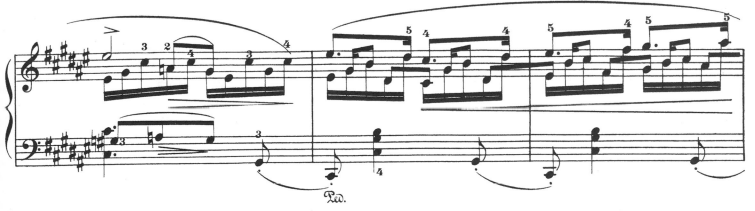

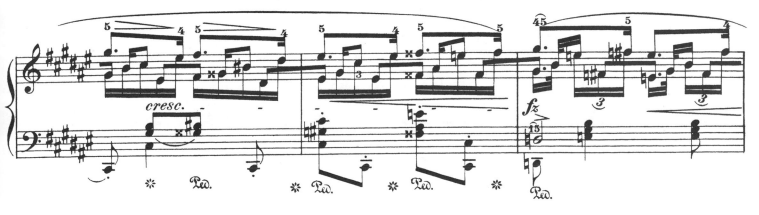

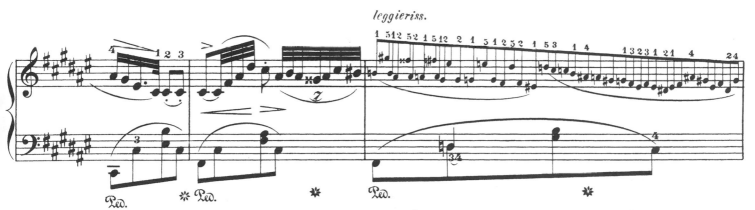

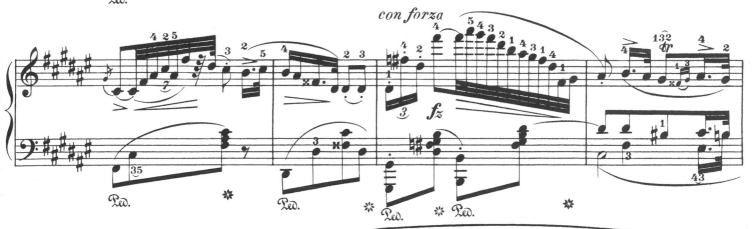

à Monsieur Ferdinand Hiller

NOCTURNE
in G minor

Frédéric Chopin
Op. 15, No. 3

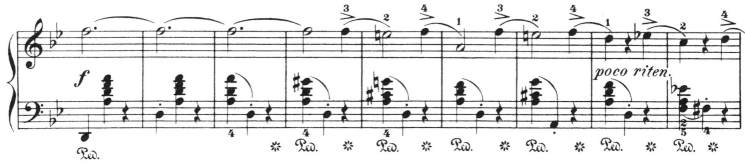

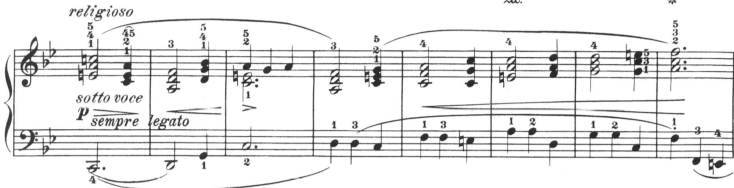

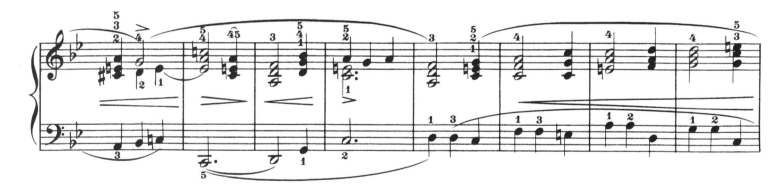

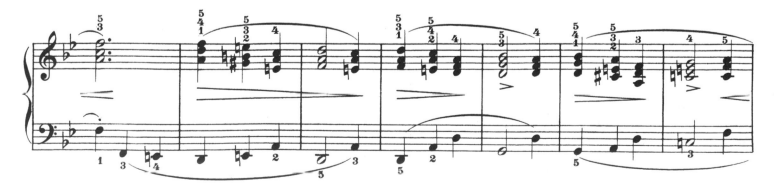

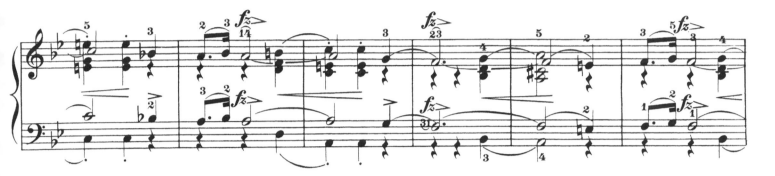

à Madame la Baronne de Billing, née de Courbonne

NOCTURNE

in B Major

Frédéric Chopin
Op. 32, No. 1

Andante sostenuto

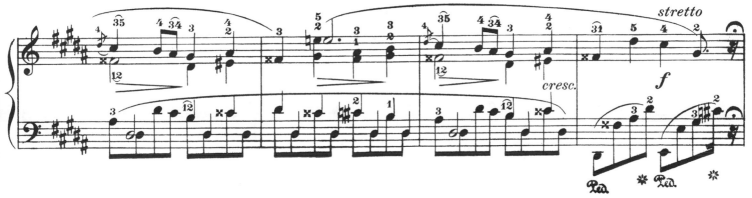

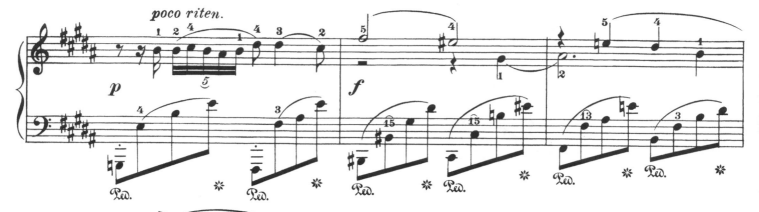

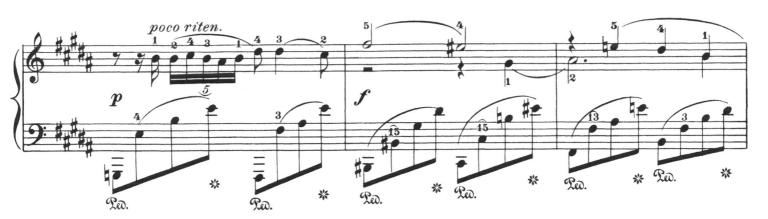

à Madame la Baronne de Billing, née de Courbonne

NOCTURNE
in A-flat Major

Frédéric Chopin
Op. 32, No. 2

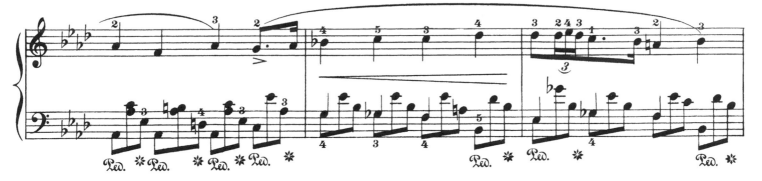

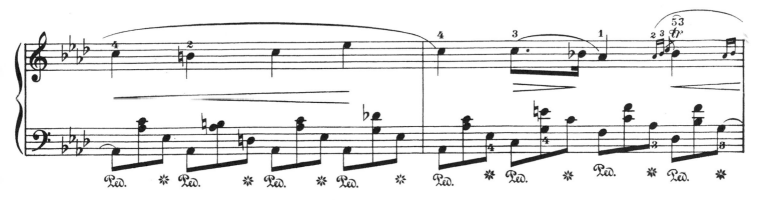

22

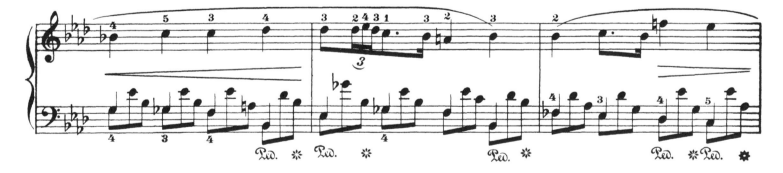

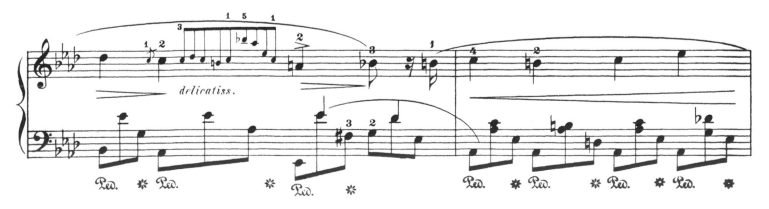

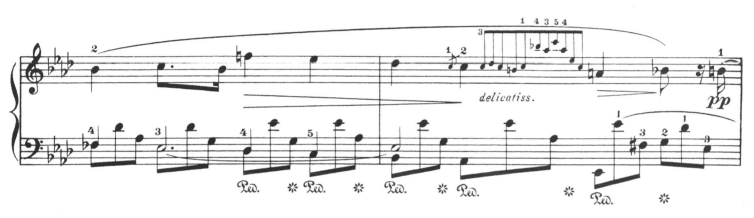

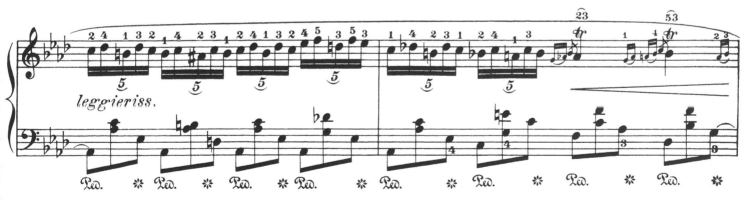

NOCTURNE
in G minor

Frédéric Chopin
Op. 37, No. 1

Andante sostenuto

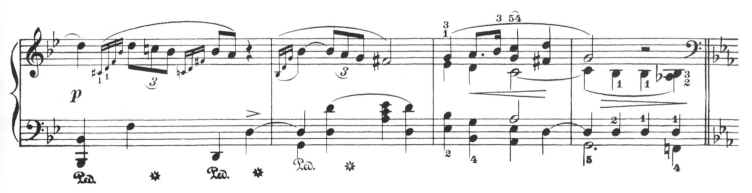

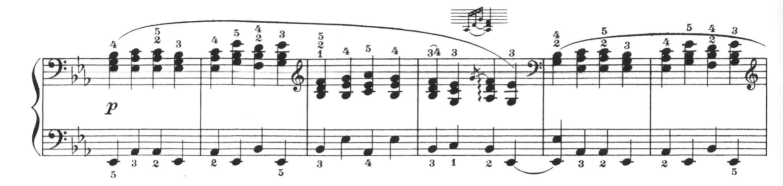

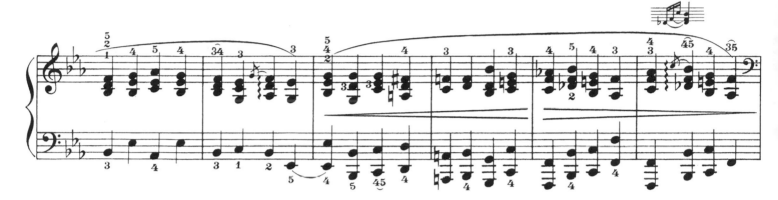

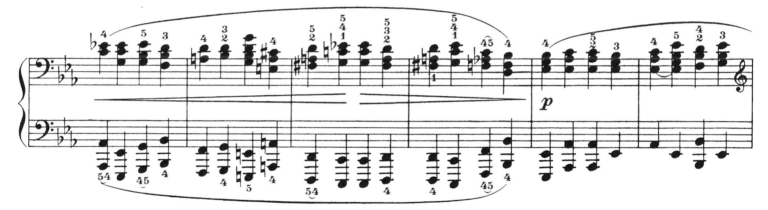

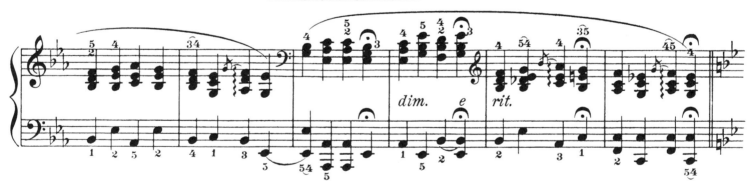

29

NOCTURNE
in G Major

Frédéric Chopin
Op. 37, No. 2

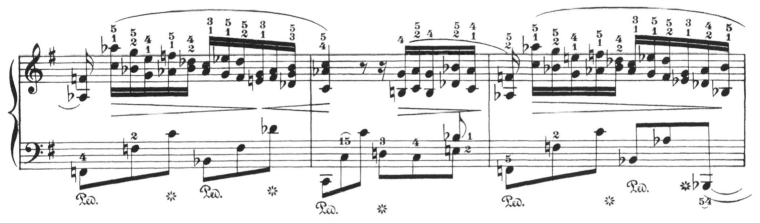

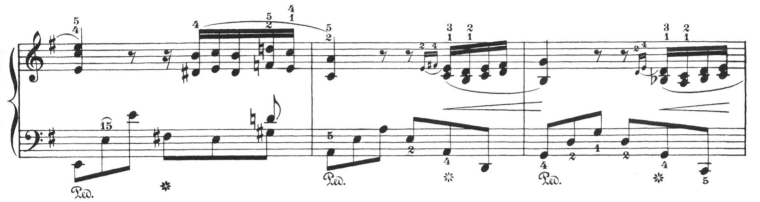

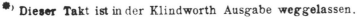

*) Dieser Takt ist in der Klindworth Ausgabe weggelassen.

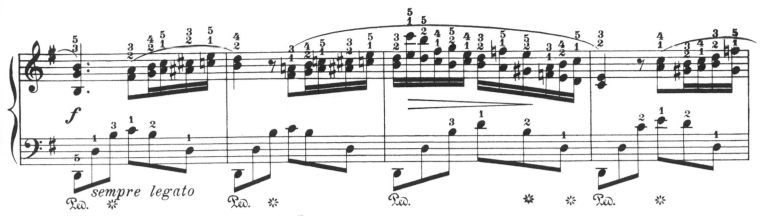

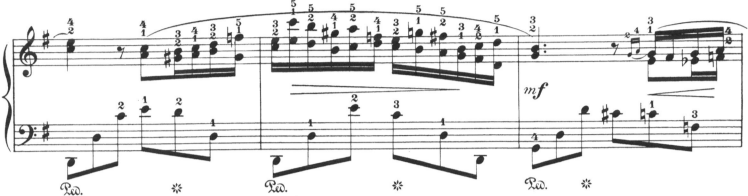

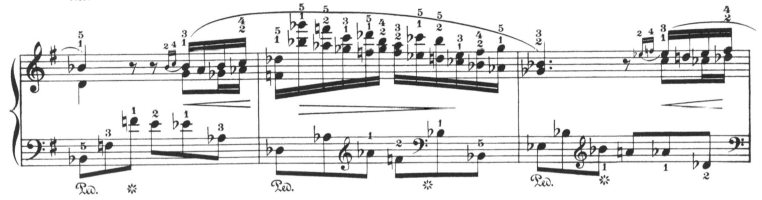

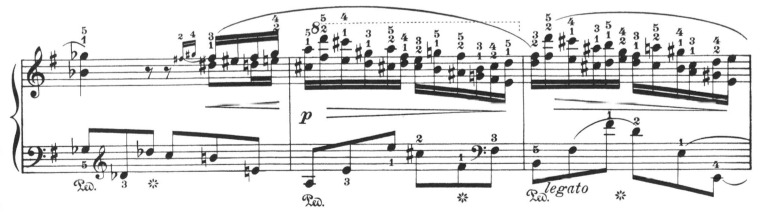

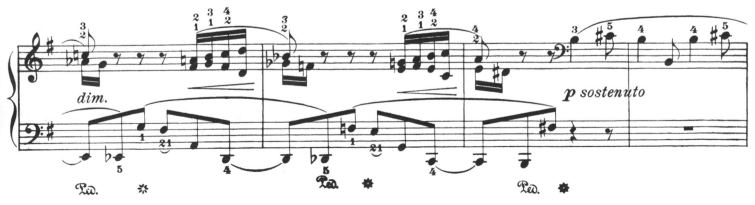

à Mademoiselle Laura Duperré

NOCTURNE
in C minor

Frédéric Chopin
Op. 48, No. 1

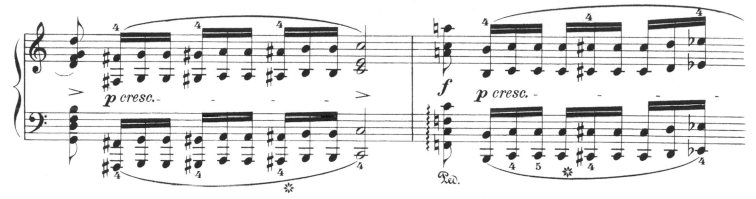

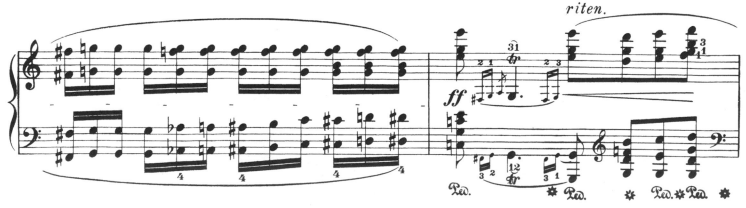

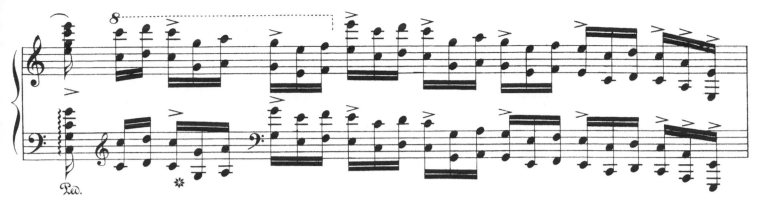

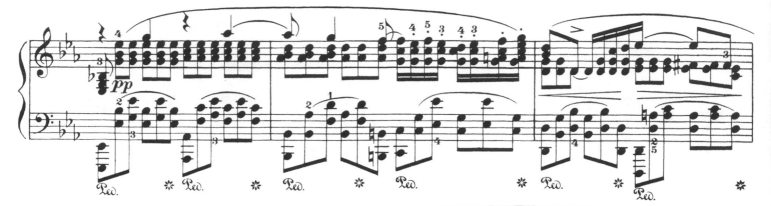

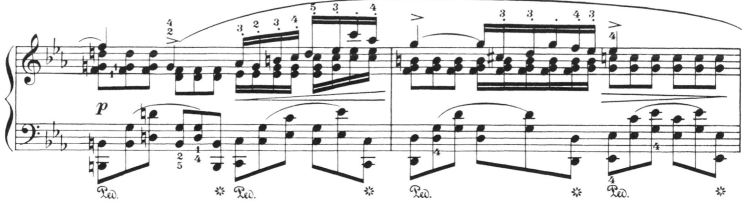

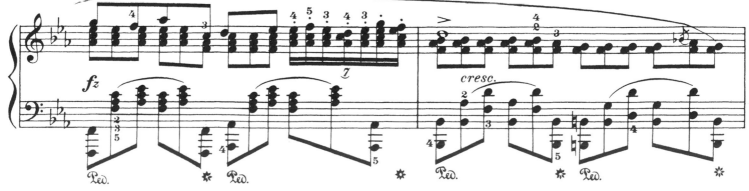

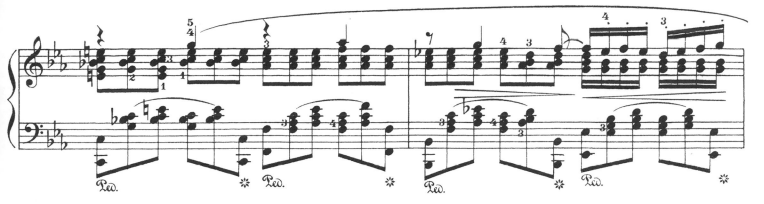

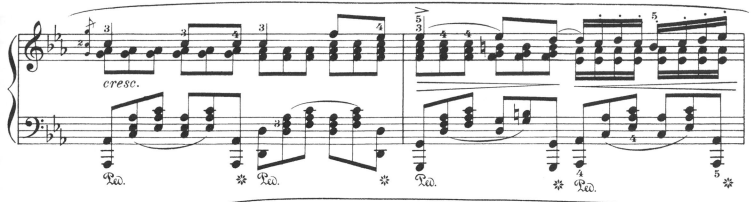

à *Mademoiselle J.W. Stirling*

NOCTURNE
in F minor

Frédéric Chopin
Op. 55, No. 1

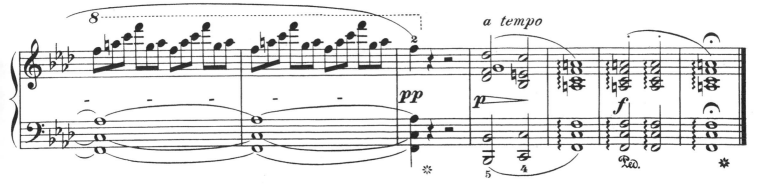

NOCTURNE
in E minor

Frédéric Chopin
Op. 72, No. 1
(Posthumous)

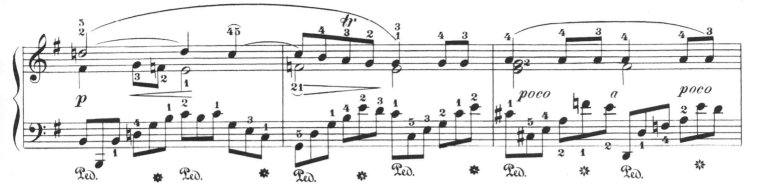

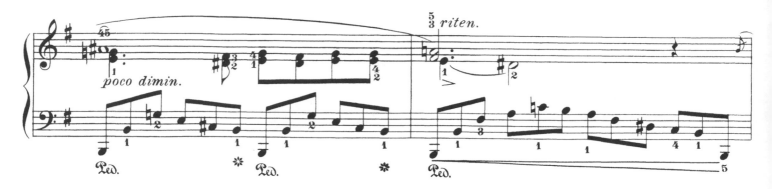

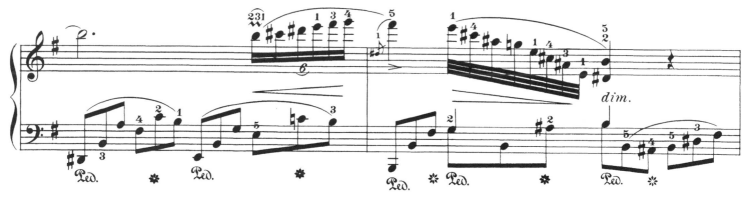

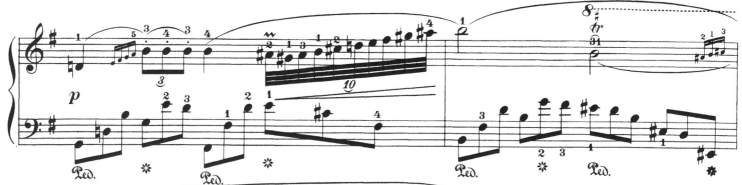

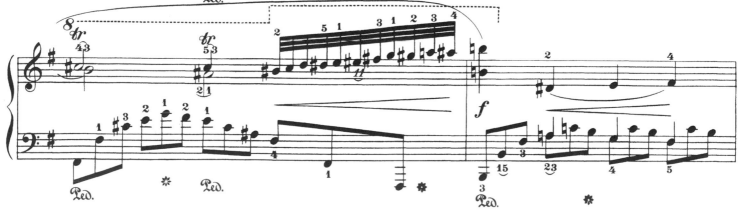

NOCTURNE
in C-sharp minor

Frédéric Chopin
Op. Posthumous

Lento con gran espressione

Tempo I

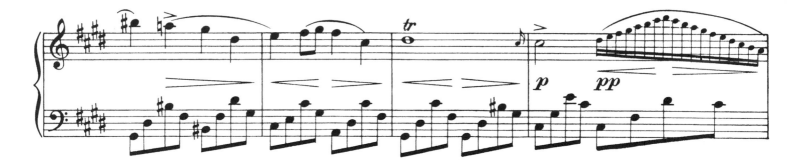

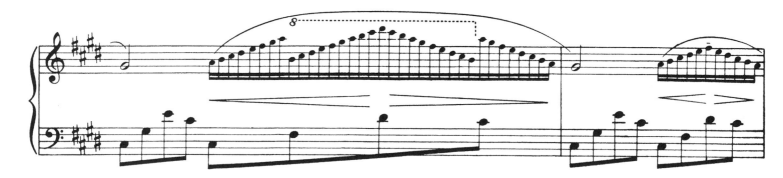

NOCTURNE
in C minor

Frédéric Chopin
Op. Posthumous

Andante sostenuto

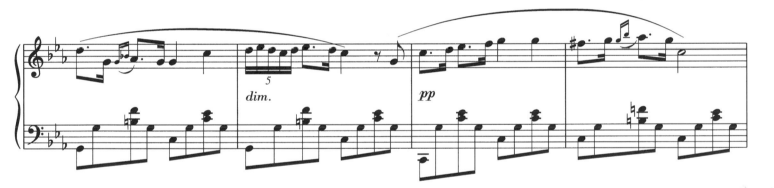

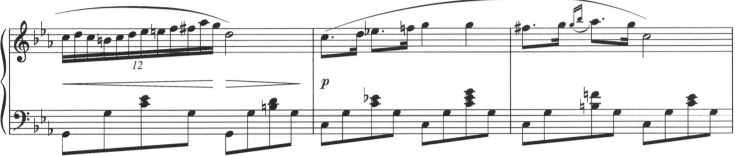

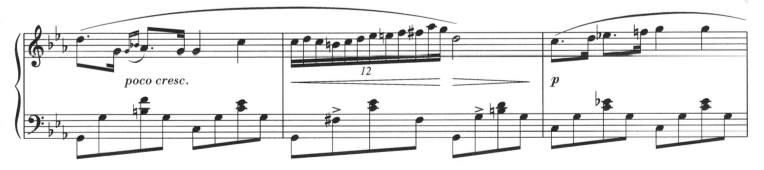

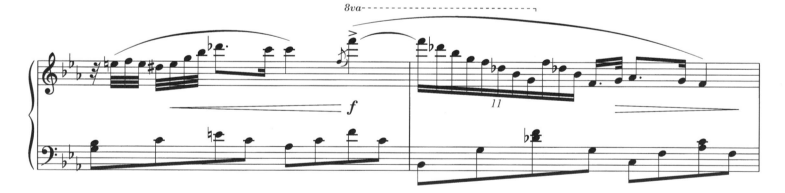

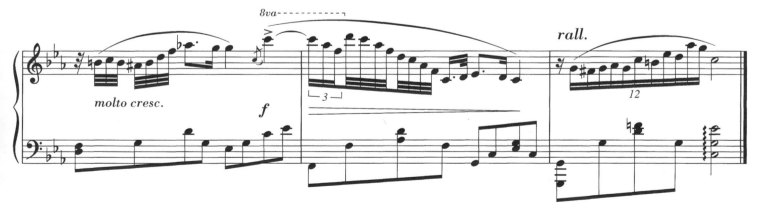

ETUDE
in E-flat minor

Frédéric Chopin
Op. 10, No. 6

sempre legatissimo

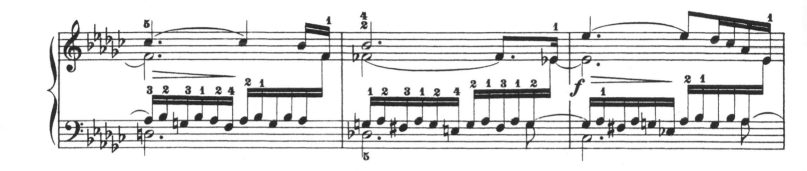

sempre legato

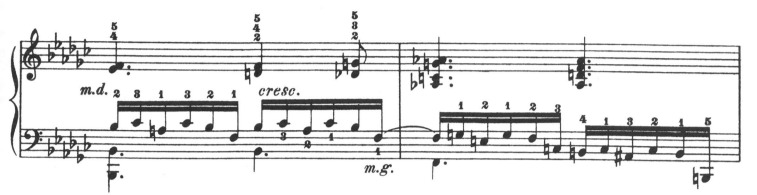

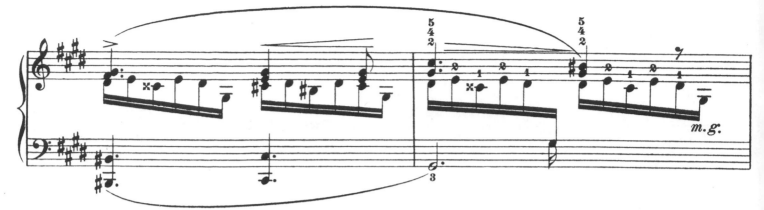

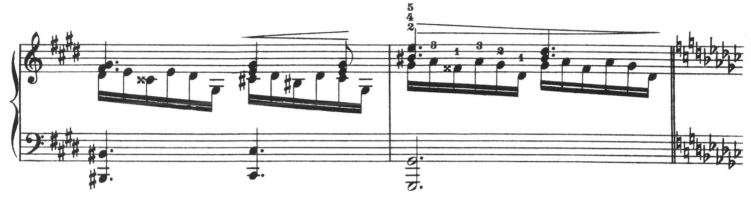

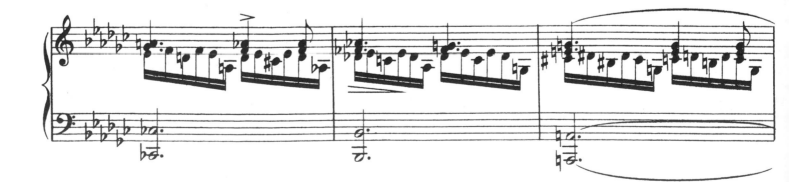

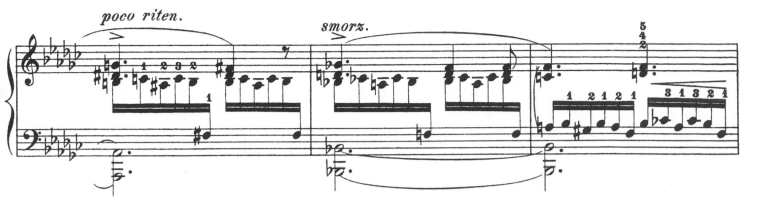

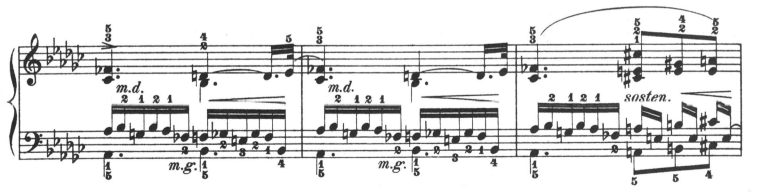

ETUDE
in F minor

Frédéric Chopin
Op. 10, No. 9

a tempo

sempre agitato

sempre legato

con forza.

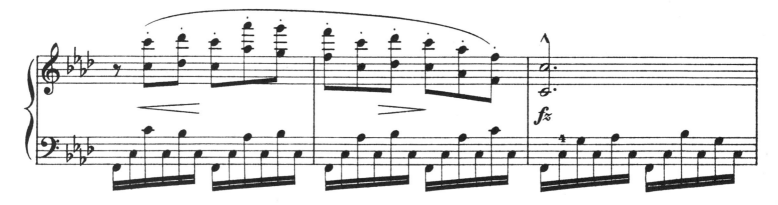

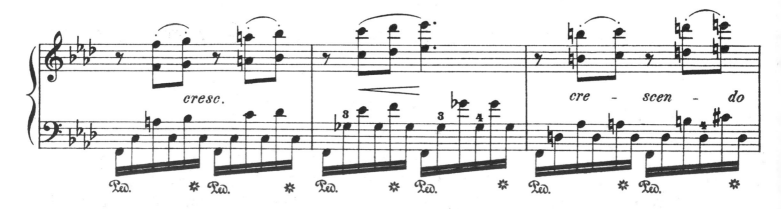

cresc.

cre - scen - do

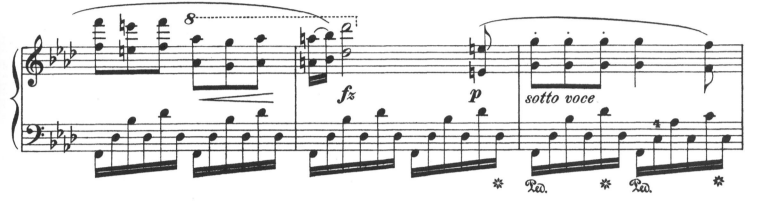

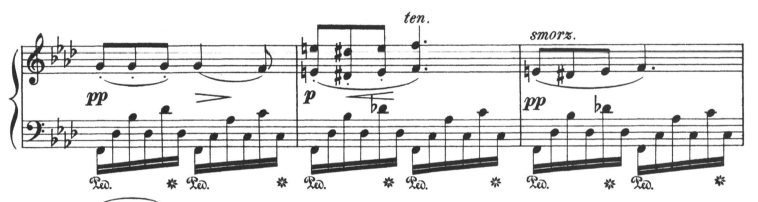

ETUDE
in C-sharp minor

Frédéric Chopin
Op. 25, No. 7

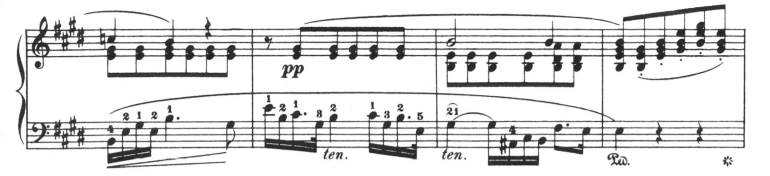

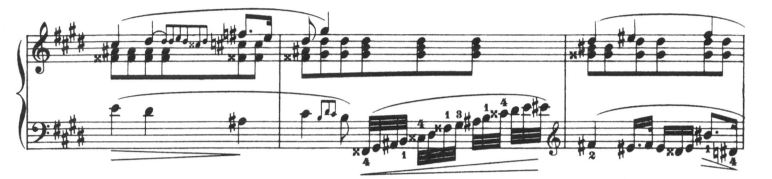

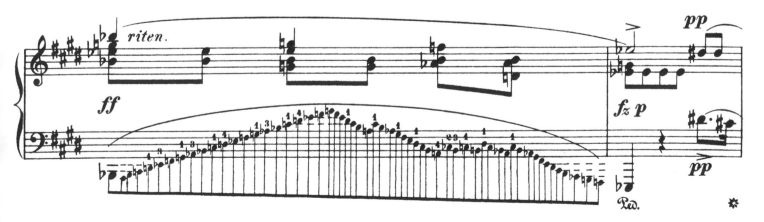

ETUDE
in G-flat Major

Frédéric Chopin
Op. 25, No. 9

TROIS NOUVELLES ÉTUDES

from *Méthode des méthodes de piano*

Etude in F minor

Frédéric Chopin

Etude in A-flat Major

Etude in D-flat Major

ETUDE
in C minor "Revolutionary"

Frédéric Chopin
Op. 10, No. 12

Allegro con fuoco (♩ = 160)

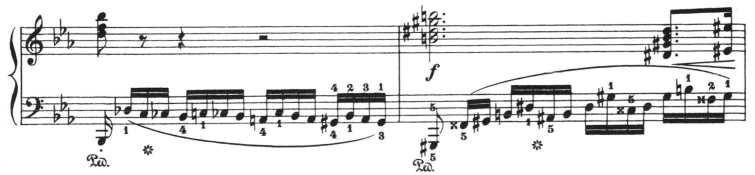

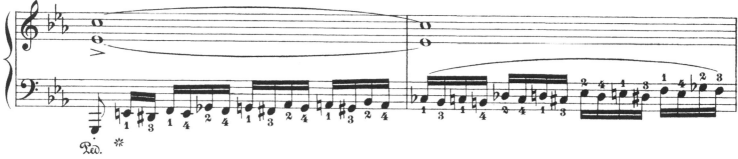

FANTAISIE-IMPROMPTU
in C-sharp minor

Revised, edited and fingered by
Rafael Joseffy

Frédéric Chopin
Op. 66 (Posthumous)

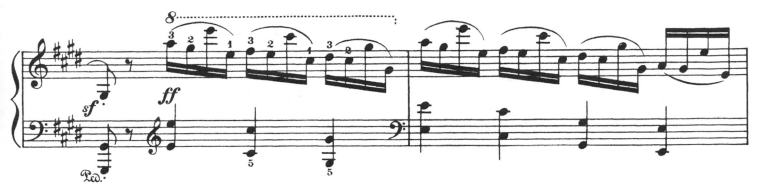

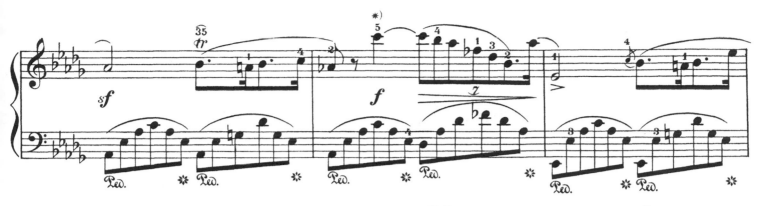

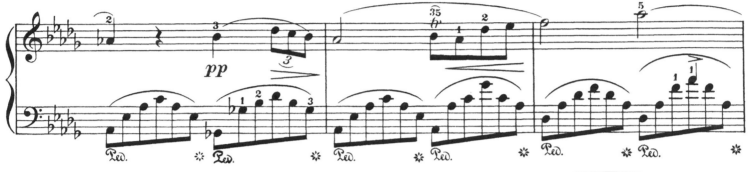

Tempo Iº (Allegro agitato)

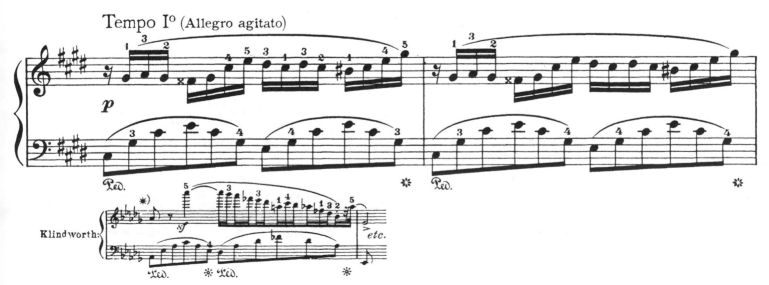

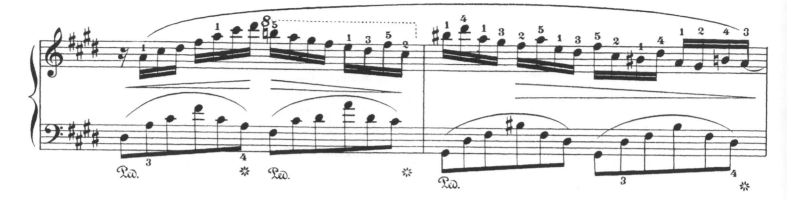

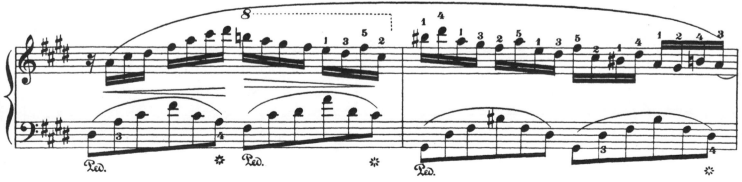

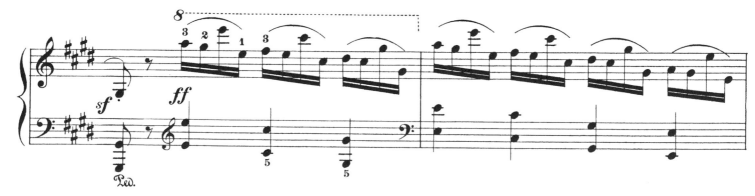

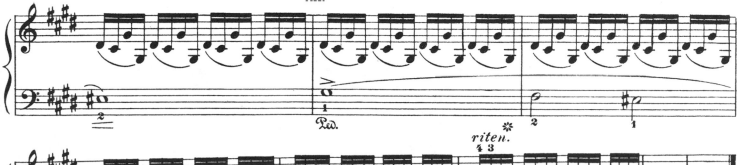

PRELUDE
in A minor

Frédéric Chopin
Op. 28, No. 2

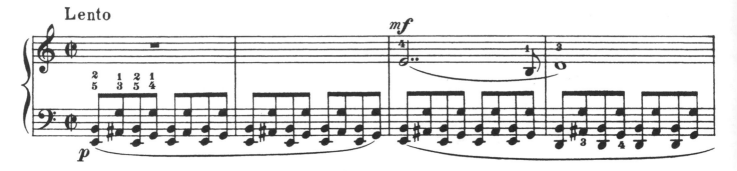

PRELUDE
in E minor

Frédéric Chopin
Op. 28, No. 4

Largo

PRELUDE
in B minor

Frédéric Chopin
Op. 28, No. 6

Lento assai

p sotto voce

sostenuto

sostenuto

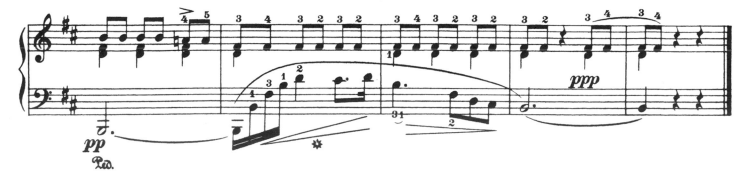

ppp

pp

PRELUDE
in E Major

Frédéric Chopin
Op. 28, No. 9

*) Scholz:

PRELUDE
in F-sharp Major

Frédéric Chopin
Op. 28, No. 13

PRELUDE
in A-flat Major

Frédéric Chopin
Op. 28, No. 17

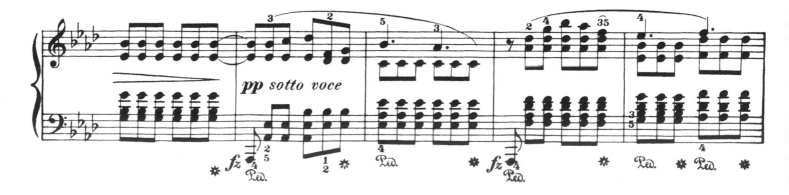

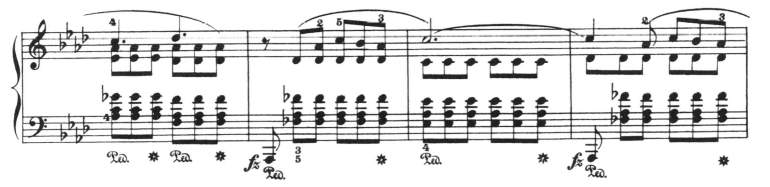

PRELUDE

in D-flat Major "Raindrop"

Frédéric Chopin
Op. 28, No. 15

Sostenuto

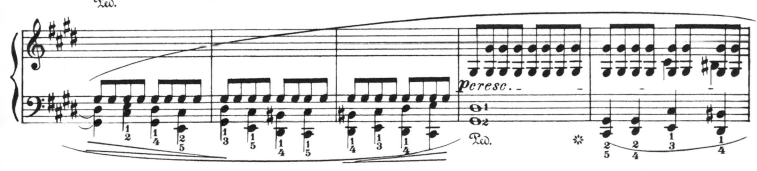

PRELUDE
in C minor

Frédéric Chopin
Op. 28, No. 20

PRELUDE
in B-flat Major

Frédéric Chopin
Op. 28, No. 21

PRELUDE
in G minor

Frédéric Chopin
Op. 28, No. 22

Molto agitato

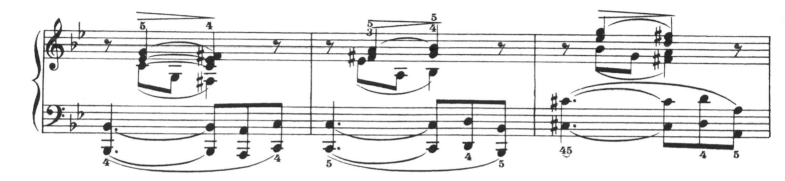

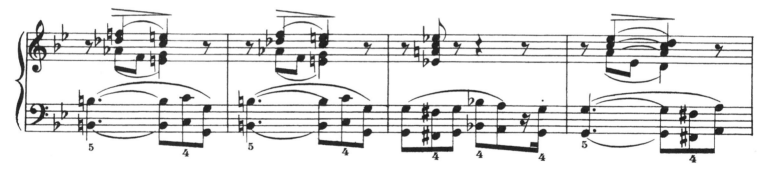

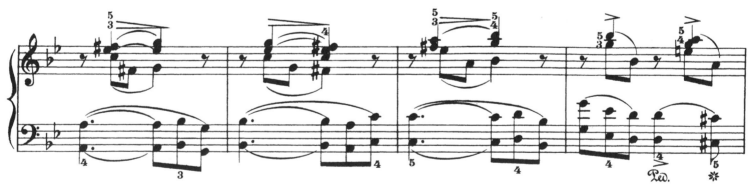

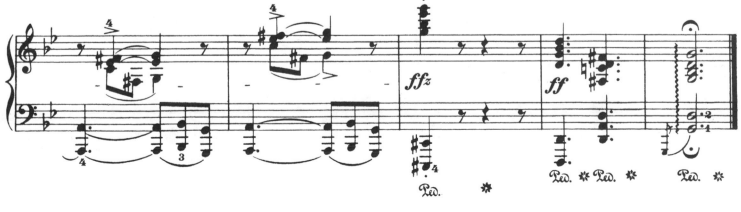

à Laura Harsford

GRAND VALSE BRILLANTE

in E-flat Major

Frédéric Chopin
Op. 18

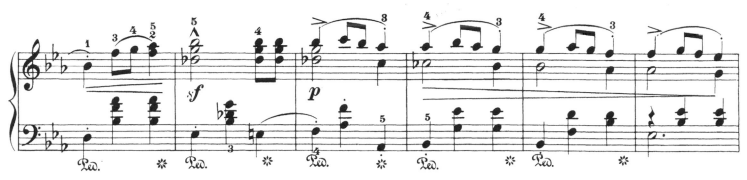

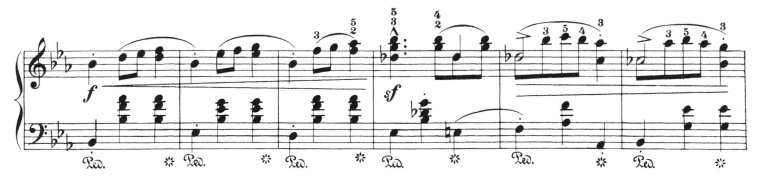

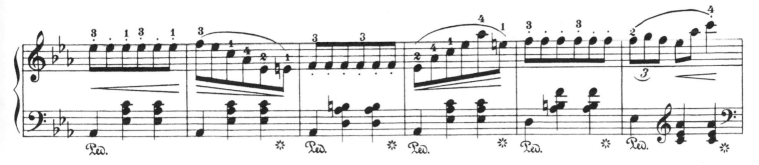

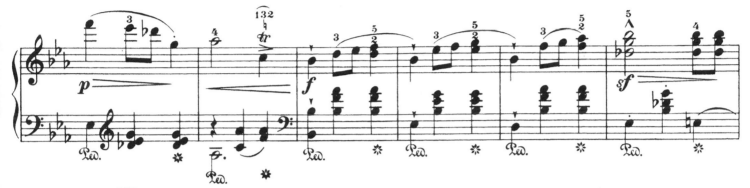

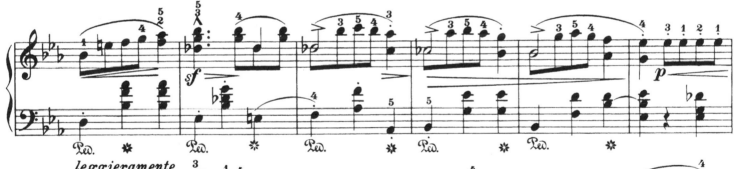

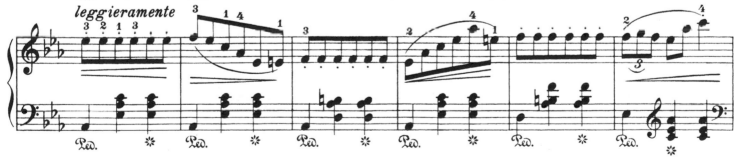

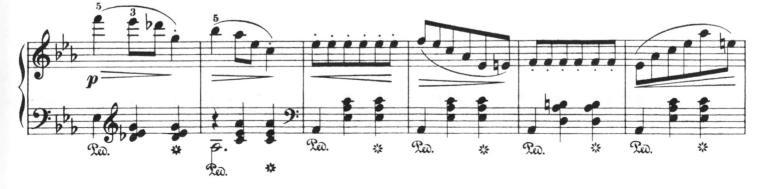

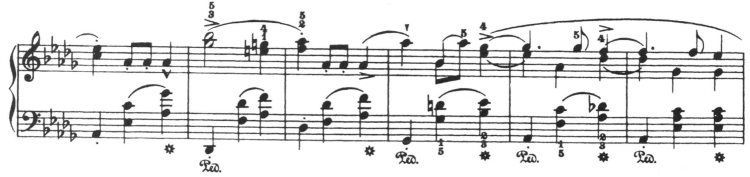

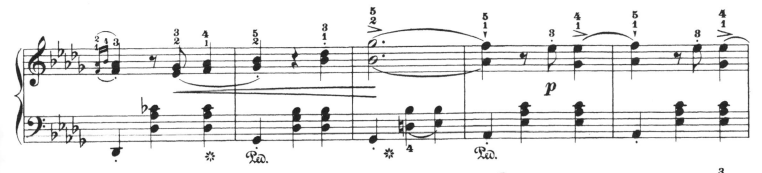

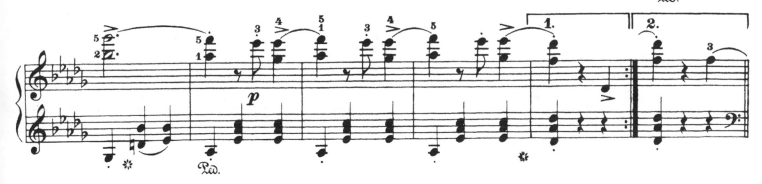

à Madame G. d'Ivry

VALSE BRILLANTE
in A minor

Frédéric Chopin
Op. 34, No. 2

Sostenuto

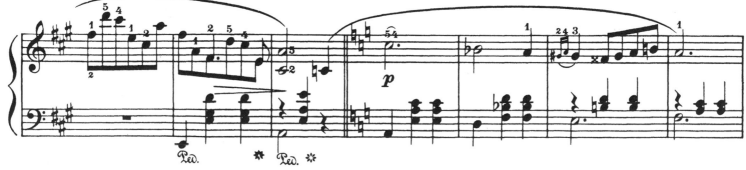

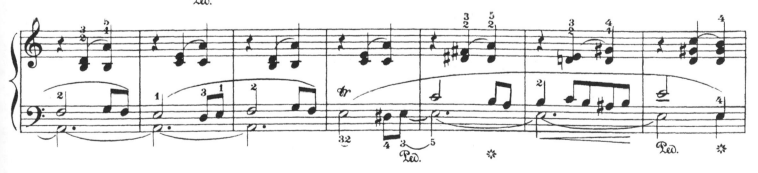

à Mademoiselle A. d'Eichthal

VALSE BRILLANTE
in F Major

Frédéric Chopin
Op. 34, No. 3

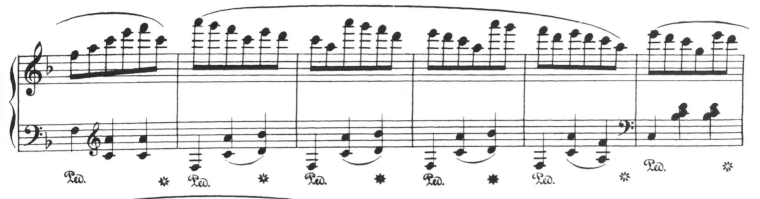

à Madame la Comtesse Delphine Potocka

WALTZ

in D-flat Major "Minute"

Frédéric Chopin
Op. 64, No. 1

à Madame Nathaniel de Rothschild

WALTZ
in C-sharp minor

Frédéric Chopin
Op. 64, No. 2

Più mosso

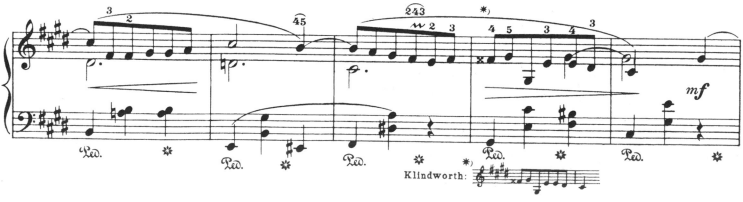

Klindworth:

WALTZ
in A-flat Major

Frédéric Chopin
Op. 69, No. 1
(Posthumous)

WALTZ
in B minor

Frédéric Chopin
Op. 69, No. 2
(Posthumous)

WALTZ
in F minor

Frédéric Chopin
Op. 70, No. 2
(Posthumous)

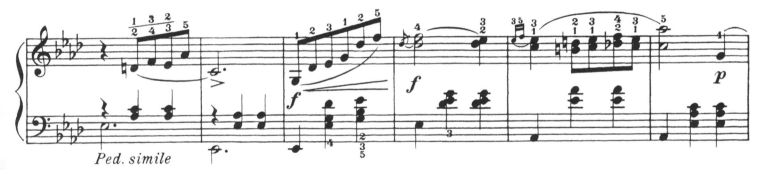

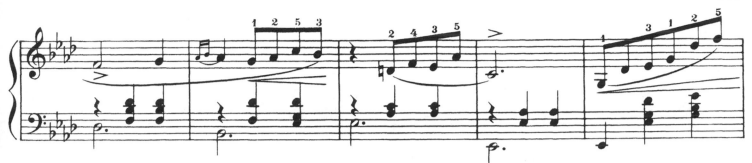

WALTZ
in E minor

Frédéric Chopin
Op. Posthumous

Vivace

WALTZ
in A minor

Frédéric Chopin
Op. Posthumous

Allegretto

à la Comtesse Katharina Bronicka

WALTZ
in A-flat Major

Frédéric Chopin
Op. 64, No. 3

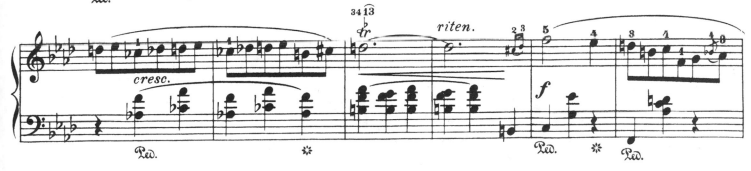

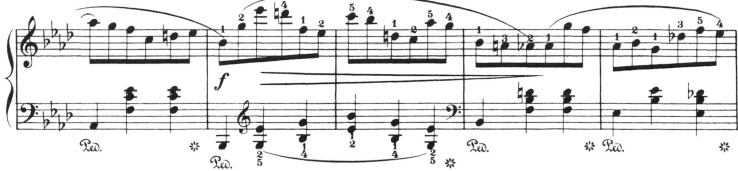

poco a poco accel. al fine

WALTZ
in E-flat Major

Frédéric Chopin
Op. Posthumous

Sostenuto

à Mademoiselle la Comtesse de Lobau

IMPROMPTU
in A-flat Major

Revised and fingered by
Rafael Joseffy

Frédéric Chopin
Op. 29

Allegro assai, quasi presto

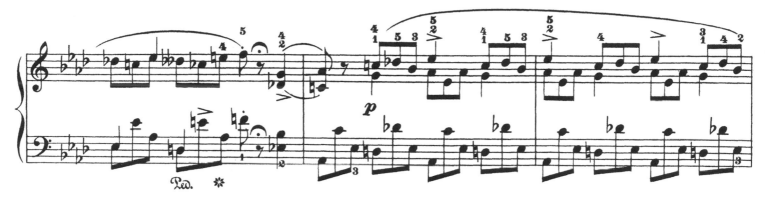

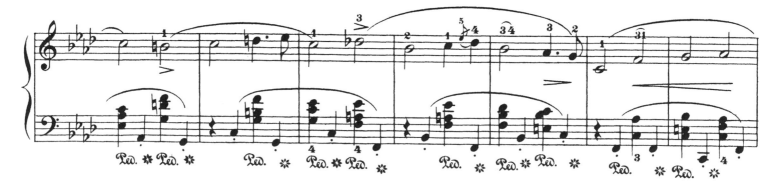

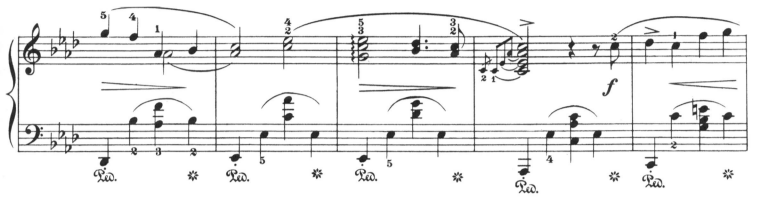

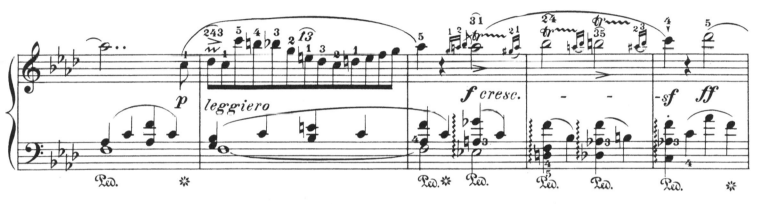

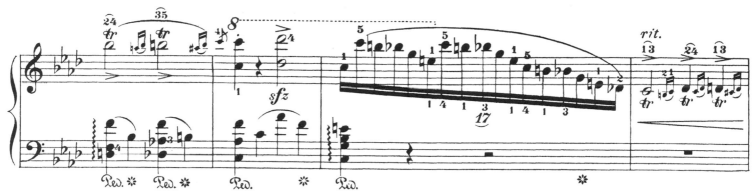

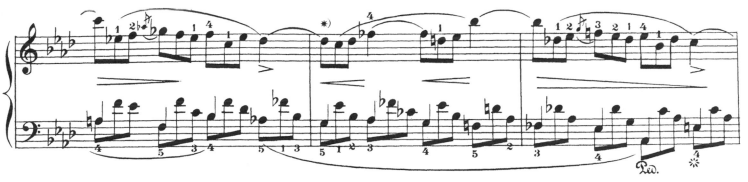

à Mademoiselle la Comtessa Pauline Plater

MAZURKA
in F-sharp minor

Frédéric Chopin
Op. 6, No. 1

Revised and fingered by
Rafael Joseffy

à Monsieur Johns de la Nouvelle-Orléans

MAZURKA
in B-flat Major

Revised and fingered by
Rafael Joseffy

Frédéric Chopin
Op. 7, No. 1

Revised and fingered by
Rafael Joseffy

MAZURKA
in A Major

Frédéric Chopin
Op. 7, No. 2

Vivo, ma non troppo (♩ = 160)

D. C. al Fine

MAZURKA
in E minor

Revised and fingered by
Rafael Joseffy

Frédéric Chopin
Op. 17, No. 2

Lento, ma non troppo (♩ = 144)

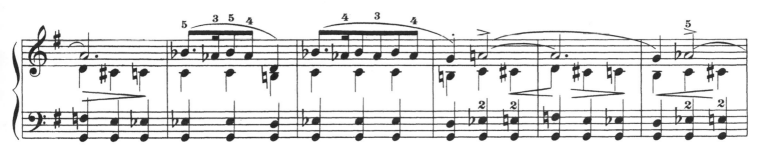

MAZURKA

in A minor

Revised and fingered by
Rafael Joseffy

Frédéric Chopin
Op. 17, No. 4

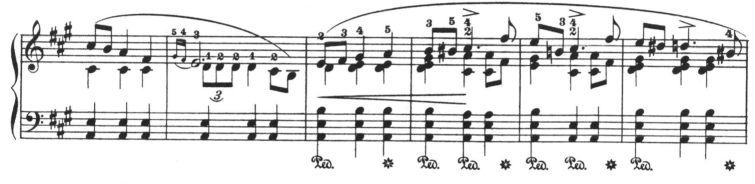

à Monsieur le Comte de Perthuis

MAZURKA
in G minor

Revised and fingered by
Rafael Joseffy

Frédéric Chopin
Op. 24, No. 1

25503

Revised and fingered by
Rafael Joseffy

MAZURKA
in B minor

Frédéric Chopin
Op. 30, No. 2

MAZURKA
in C Major

Revised and fingered by
Rafael Joseffy

Frédéric Chopin
Op. 33, No. 3

Semplice

MAZURKA
in F minor

Revised and fingered by
Rafael Joseffy

Frédéric Chopin
Op. 63, No. 2

MAZURKA
in G minor

Revised and fingered by
Rafael Joseffy

Frédéric Chopin
Op. 67, No. 2
(Posthumous)

MAZURKA
in C Major

Revised and fingered by
Rafael Joseffy

Frédéric Chopin
Op. 67, No. 3
(Posthumous)

Revised and fingered by
Rafael Joseffy

MAZURKA
in A minor

Frédéric Chopin
Op. 67, No. 4
(Posthumous)

MAZURKA
in A minor

Revised and fingered by
Rafael Joseffy

Frédéric Chopin
Op. 68, No. 2
(Posthumous)

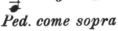

MAZURKA
in F Major

Frédéric Chopin
Op. 68, No. 3
(Posthumous)

Revised and fingered by
Rafael Joseffy

Allegro, ma non troppo (♩ = 132)

MAZURKA
in F minor

Frédéric Chopin
Op. 68, No. 4
(Posthumous)

Revised and fingered by
Rafael Joseffy

Dal segno senza fine

MAZURKA
in C Major

Revised and fingered by
Rafael Joseffy

Frédéric Chopin
Op. 7, No. 5

Dal Segno senza Fine

MARCHE FUNÈBRE

from Piano Sonata No. 2 in B-flat minor

Frédéric Chopin
Op. 35

à Monsieur Joseph Dessauer

POLONAISE

in C-sharp minor

Frédéric Chopin
Op. 26, No. 1

Allegro appassionato

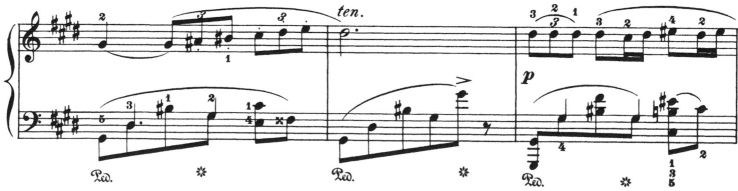

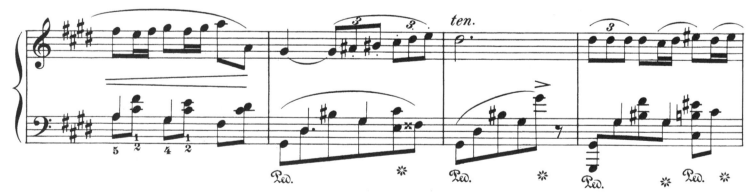

Fine

meno mosso

con anima

Polonaise da Capo al Fine

à Monsieur Julian Fontana

POLONAISE
in A Major "Military"

Frédéric Chopin
Op. 40, No. 1

Allegro con brio

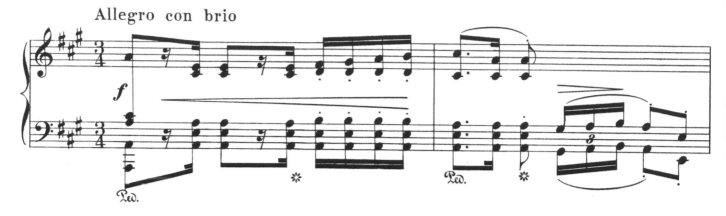

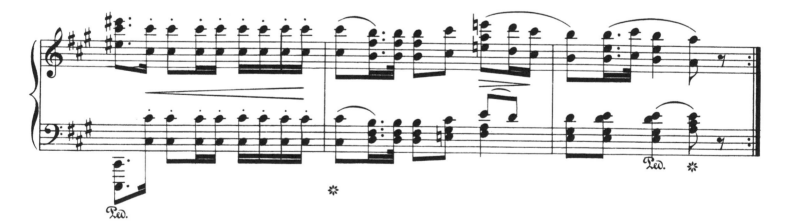

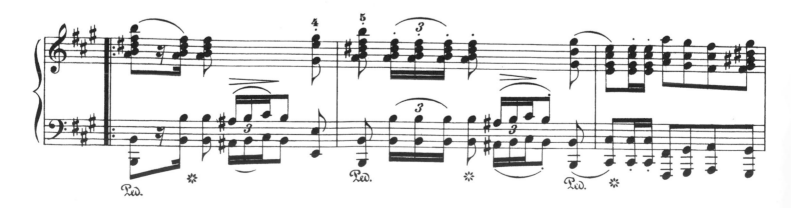

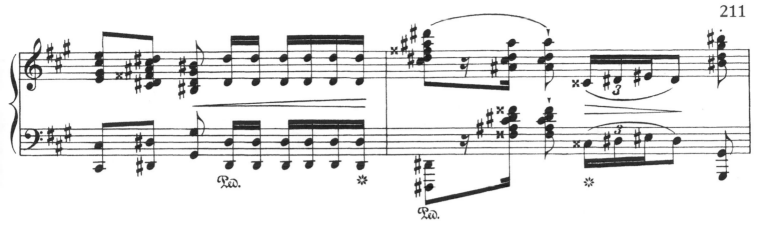

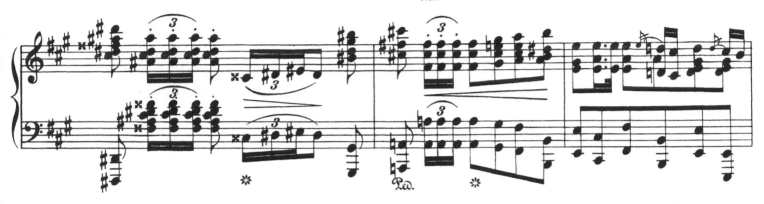

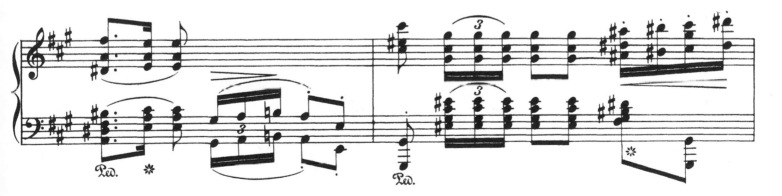

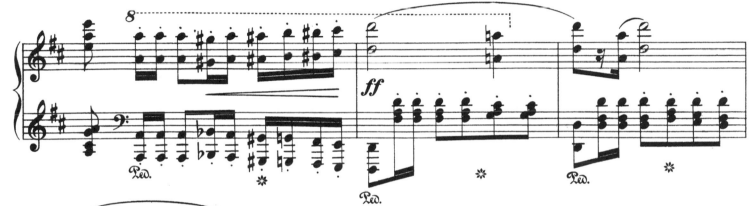

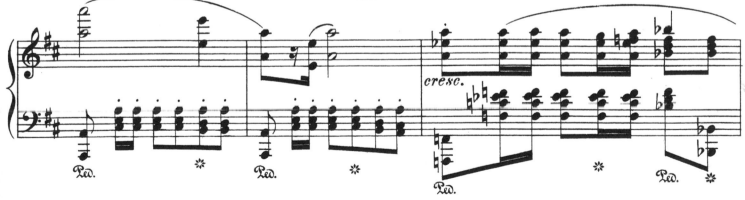

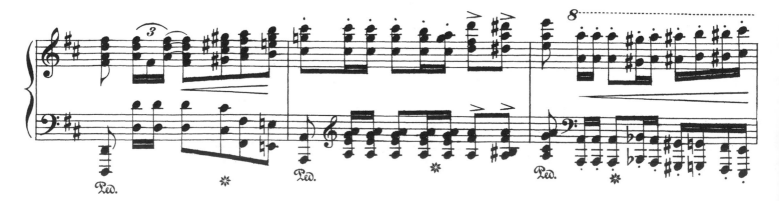

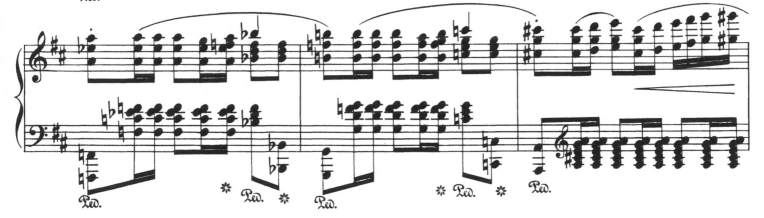

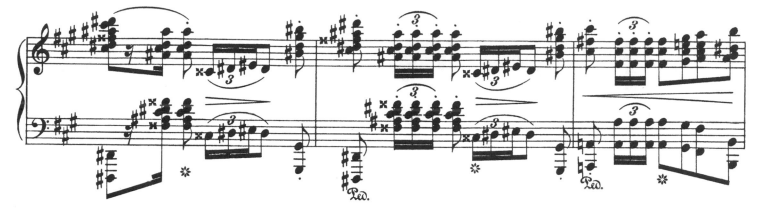

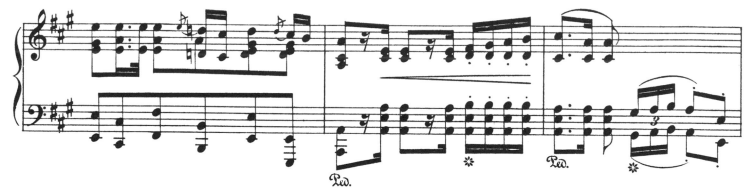

POLONAISE
in C minor

Frédéric Chopin
Op. 40, No. 2

Allegro maestoso

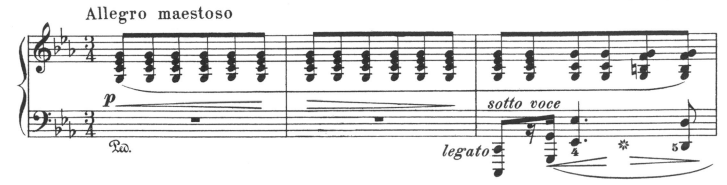

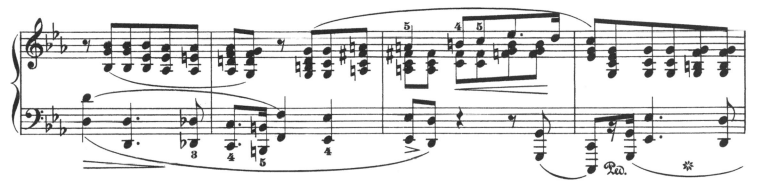

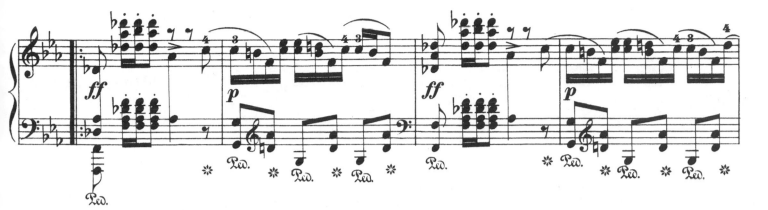

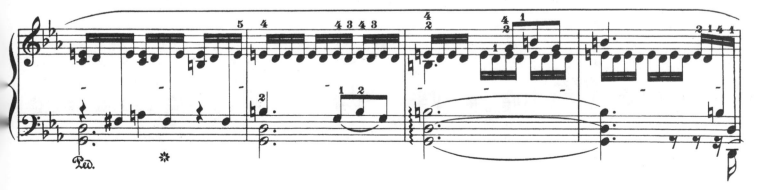

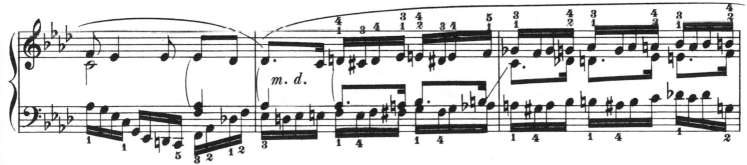

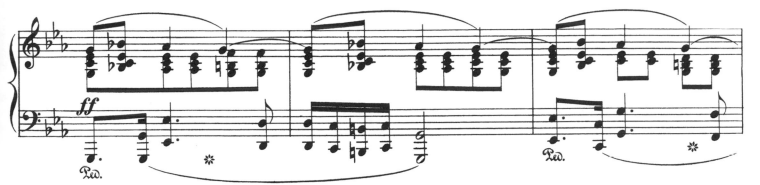

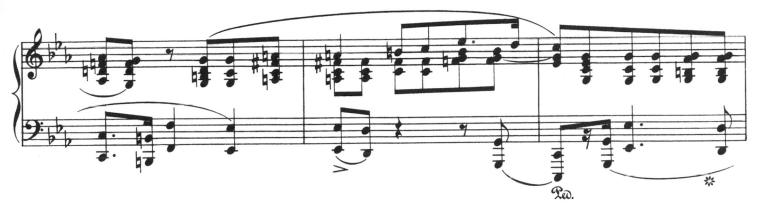

à Mademoiselle la Comtessa de Fürstenstein

SCHERZO
in D-flat Major

Edited and fingered by
Rafael Joseffy

Frédéric Chopin
Op. 31

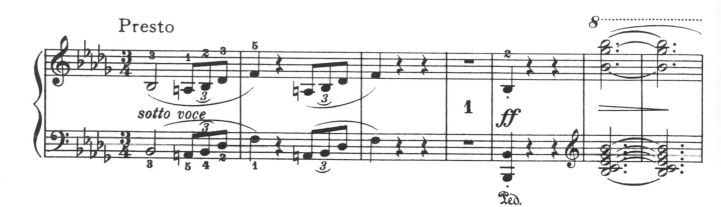

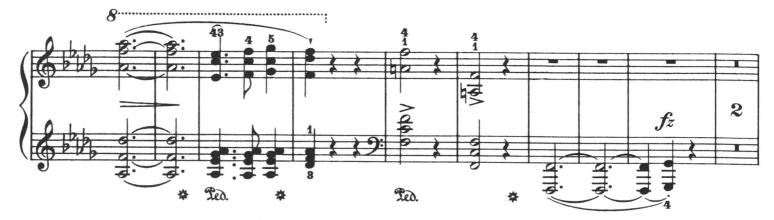

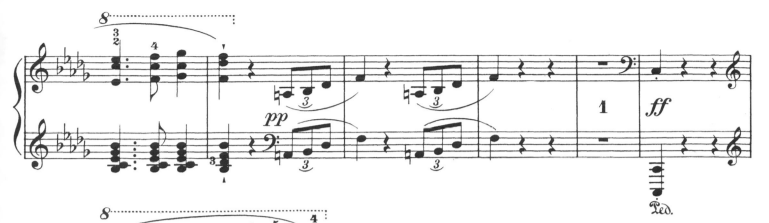
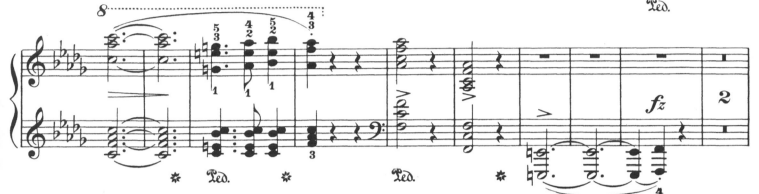
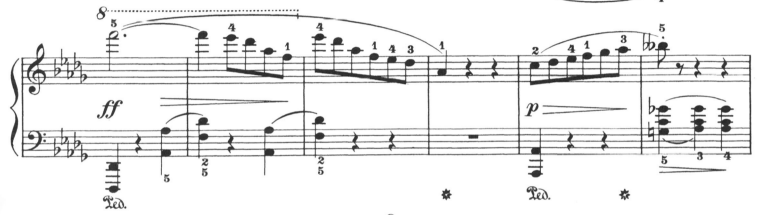
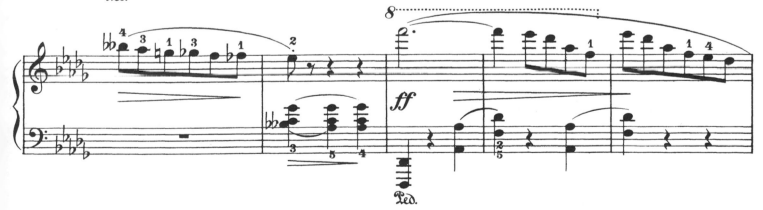

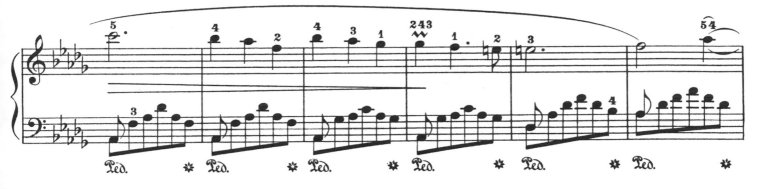

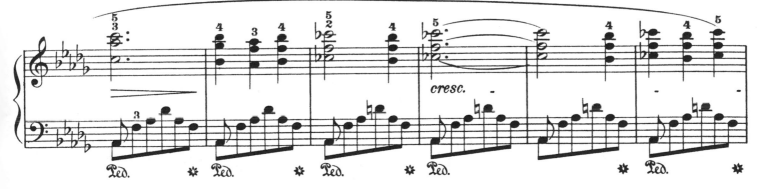

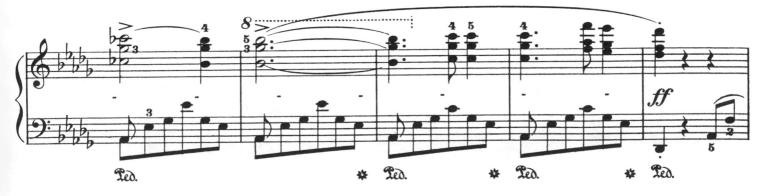

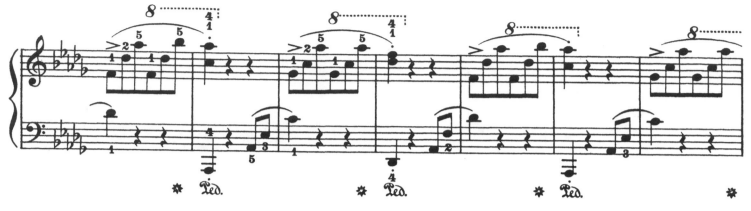

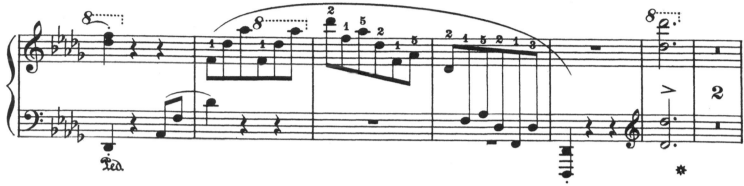

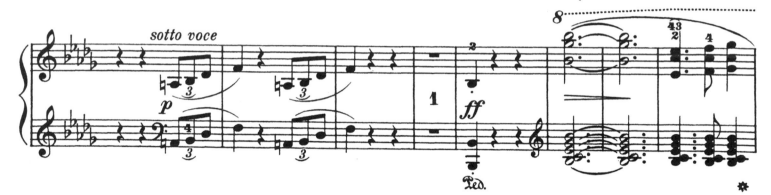

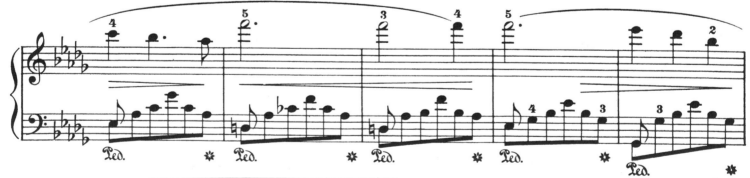

232

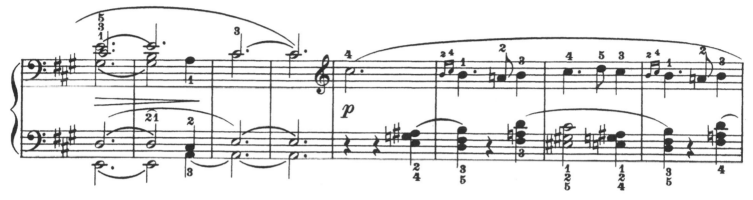

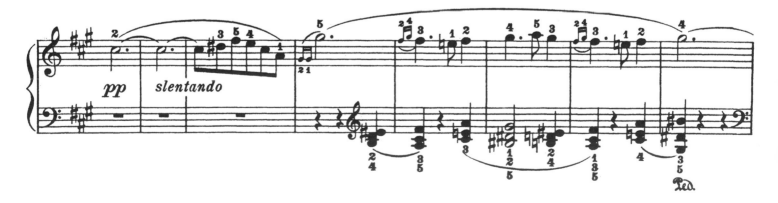

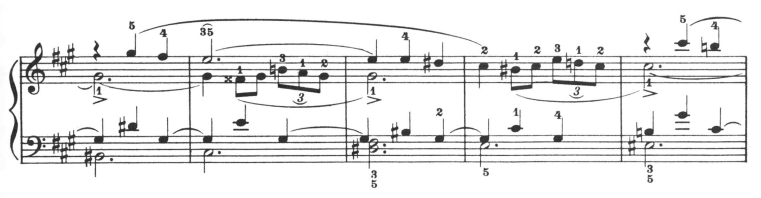

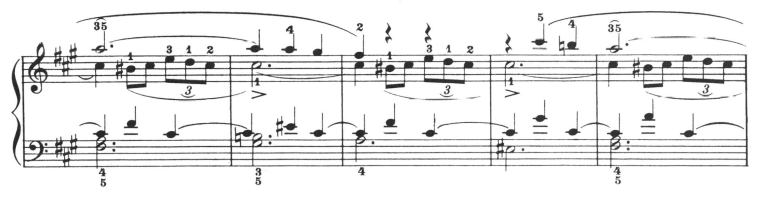

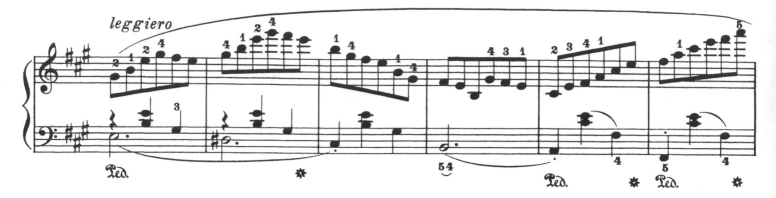

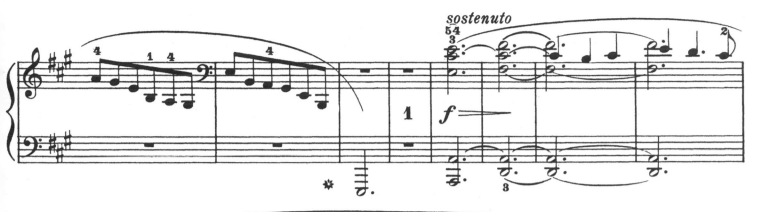

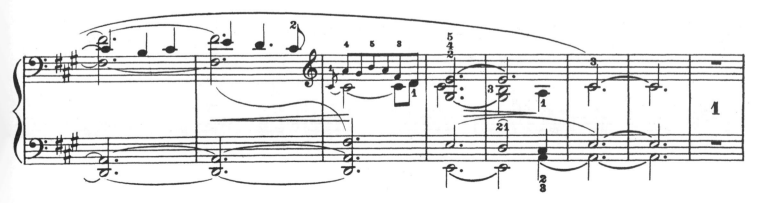

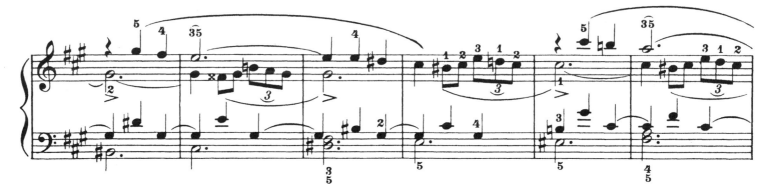

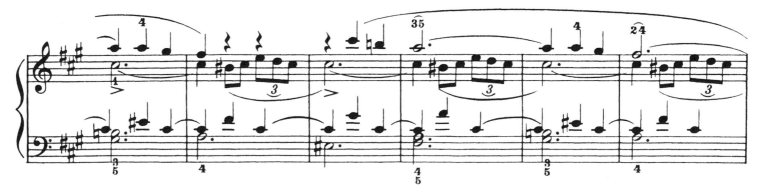

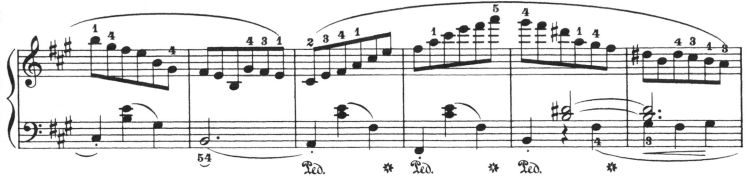

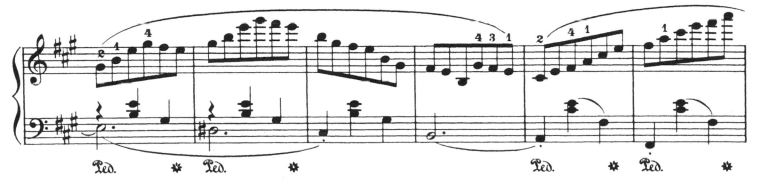

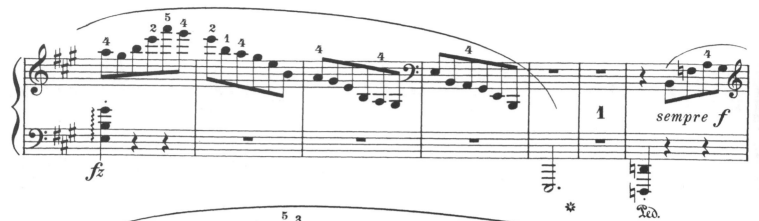

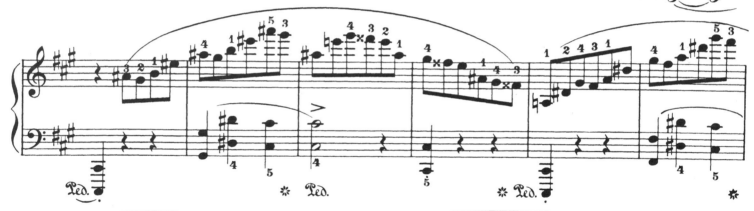

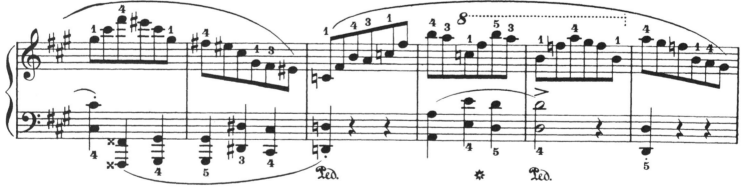

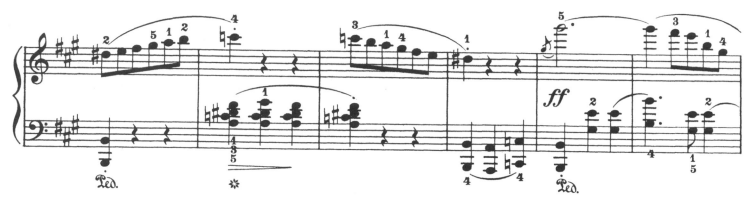

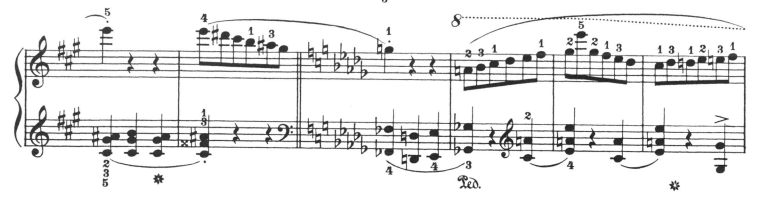

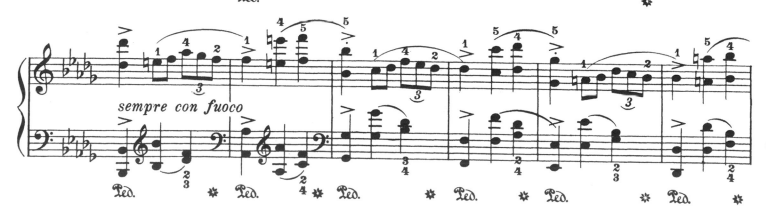

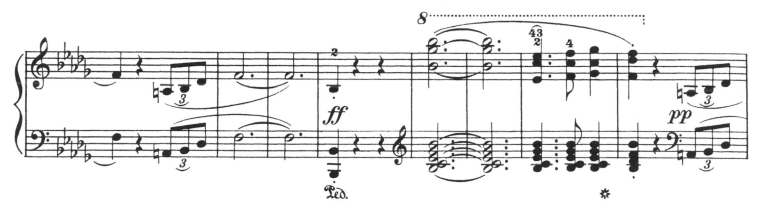

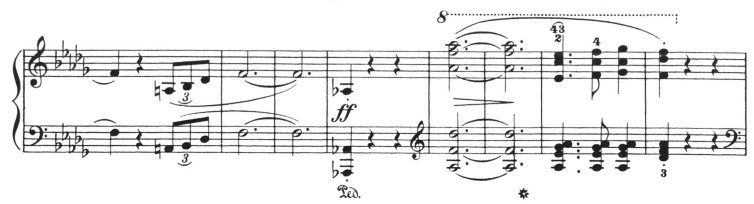

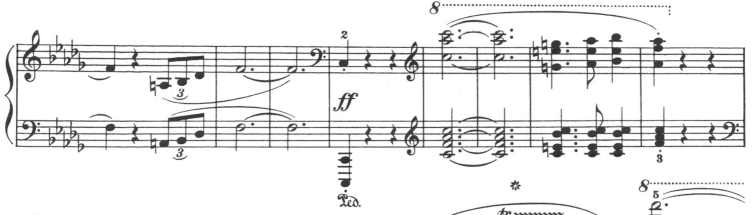

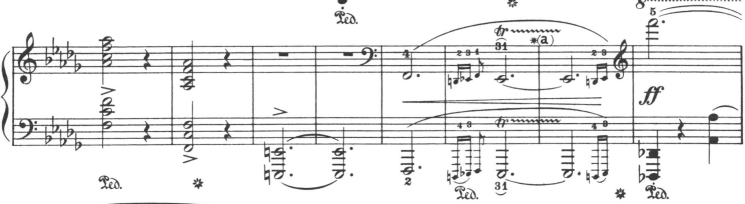

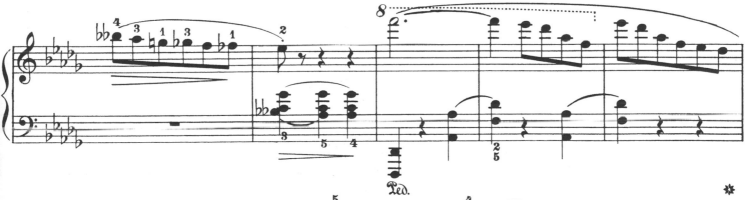

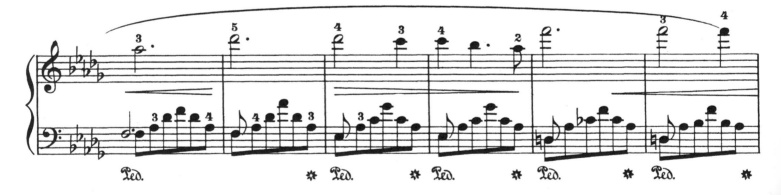

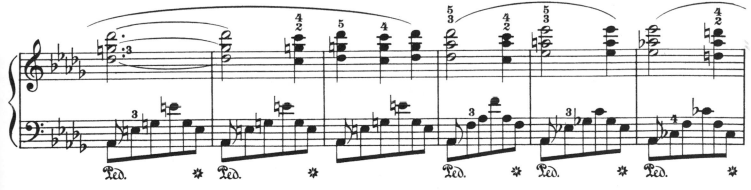

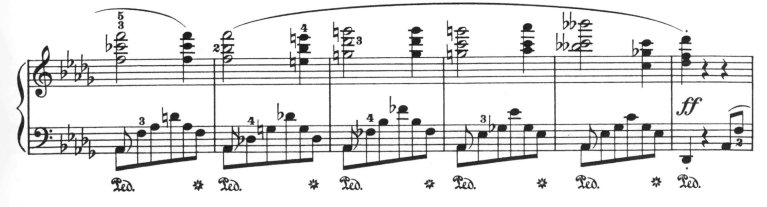

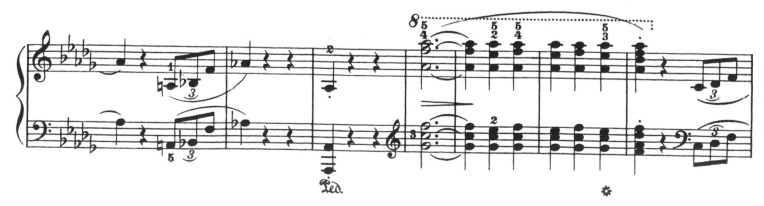

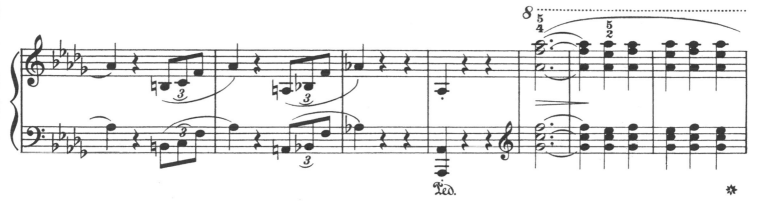

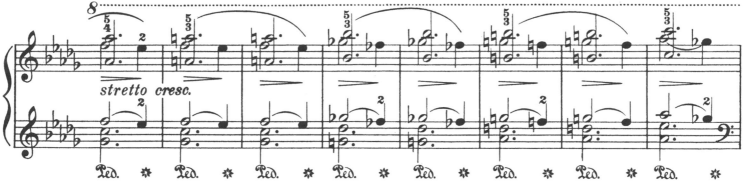

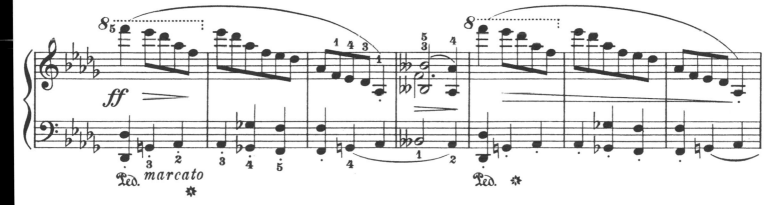

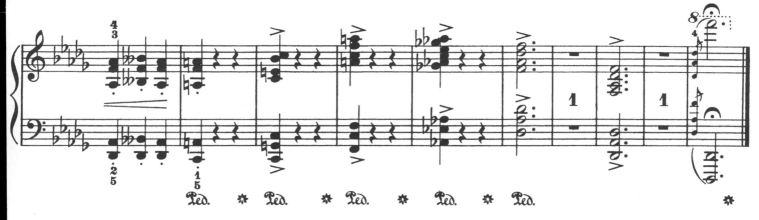